Unit 9

How Things Change

Mc
Graw
Hill
Education

Contents

Jake Made Cake

Jake said, "Dad, can I help?
I can bake cake for Pop!"
Dad said, "Yes, Jake.
You can make it."

Jake said, "Mom, can I take this?"
Mom said, "Yes, Jake.
Save the box."

Jake made a cake box.
Jake made it red, too.
It had a name on it.
Jake had POP on it!

Pop came late.
Pop came in the gate.
Jake ran to Pop.
Jake gave Pop cake.

Jake said, "I made cake!"
Jake and Pop ate cake.
Yum!

We Help Make It

Jane can help Dad fix
the gate.
Jane made the gate lock.
Dad made it safe, too.

Abe can help Mom
make cake.
Abe can mix it up.
Mom can bake it in a tin.

Kate can help rake.
Yes. Kate can rake a lot.
Can Dave rake, too?

Dale can help tape
up a big box.
It is a big job!
Dale can tape a lot.

Gabe can see the lake.
Can Gabe get a rock?
Yes. Nate can help take
Gabe to the lake!

Lake Time Fun

"It is a fine time to ride,"
said Ike.

"I can hike," said Mike.

Ike got on a big tan bike.
Ike can bike ride a mile.
Ike can ride five!

Mike got quite a big pack.
Mike fit in a big red kite.
Mike can hike a fun mile.

Ike can ride to a fine lake.
Mike and Ike like the big lake.
Mike and Ike have a fun time.

Mike has the big red kite.
Ike can run in the hot sun.
They play at the big fine
lake.

Pike Lane

Pike Lane

The sun is up.
Get up!
Time to pick up on
Pike Lane!

Pick up a can on Pike Lane.
It has to go in the red bin.
We pick up ten.

Pick up a pine log.
Pick up on Pike Lane!
It can go in a big bag.
We can pick up five.

Rake on Pike Lane.
Make a big pile.
Hop in the big pile!

Time to play on Pike Lane.

Get a kite.

Hop on a bike.

Pike Lane is quite fine!

24

Jo Made It At Home

Where can Jo go?
Jo can go hike. Jo can
see a lot on a hike.

A mole dug a big hole.
The mole is not home.
Jo can get a rock.

Jo can see a red rose.
The rose is on a vine.
Did Jo poke at it?
No!

Jo can get a pine cone.
Jo can take a nut.
Jo can tote it home.
Time to go home, Jo.

Jo had a big pile.
Look what Jo made.
I hope you like it!

Cole and Hope woke up.
Can we make a fake home?
Mom said yes, so time to go!

Where can they make it?
"I vote the cove," said Hope.
Cole and Hope rode in line.

Cole got a big wide log.
Hope got a fat rope.
Cole got a pole.
Hope got a red rag.

Cole made a rug.
Hope got a big pine cone.
This home can look so fine!

Cole and Hope made
a code.
Mom can jot a joke on
a note.
It can get Mom in!

Jake Made Cake   WORD COUNT: 85

DECODABLE WORDS

Target Phonics Elements
Long *a, a_e:* ate, bake, cake, came, gate, gave, Jake, late, made, make, name, save, take

HIGH-FREQUENCY WORDS

help, too
Review: a, and, for, I, said, the, this, to, you

We Help Make It   WORD COUNT: 90

DECODABLE WORDS

Target Phonics Elements
Long *a, a_e:* Abe, bake, cake, Dale, Dave, Gabe, gate, Jane, Kate, lake, made, make, Nate, rake, safe, take, tape

HIGH-FREQUENCY WORDS

help, too
Review: a, see, the, we

Lake Time Fun   WORD COUNT: 94

DECODABLE WORDS

Target Phonics Elements
Long *i, i_e:* bike, fine, five, hike, Ike, kite, Mike, mile, quite, ride, time

HIGH-FREQUENCY WORDS

has, play
Review: a, and, is, said, the, to

Pike Lane   WORD COUNT: 87

DECODABLE WORDS

Target Phonics Elements
Long *i, i_e:* bike, fine, five, kite, Pike, pile, pine, quite, time

HIGH-FREQUENCY WORDS

has, play
Review: a, go, is, the, to, we

Jo Made It At Home   WORD COUNT: 90

DECODABLE WORDS

Target Phonics Elements
Long *o, o_e, o:* cone, hole, home, hope, Jo, mole, poke, rose, go, no, so, tote

HIGH-FREQUENCY WORDS

look, where
Review: a, I, is, see, the, what, you

Joke Note   WORD COUNT: 92

DECODABLE WORDS

Target Phonics Elements
Long *o, o_e, o:* Cole, code, cone, cove, home, Hope, joke, pole, rode, rope, vote, woke

HIGH-FREQUENCY WORDS

where
Review: a, and, I, said, the, they, this, to

37

HIGH-FREQUENCY WORDS TAUGHT TO DATE

Grade K

a
and
are
can
do
for
go
has
have
he
help
here
I
is
like
little
look
me
my
of
play
said
see
she
the
they
this
to
too
want
was
we
what
where
with
you

DECODING SKILLS TAUGHT TO DATE

Initial and final consonant *m*; short *a*; initial *s*; initial and final consonant *p*; initial and final consonant *t*; initial and medial vowel *i*; initial and final consonant *n*; initial *c*; initial and medial vowel *o*; initial and final *d*; initial consonant *h*; initial and medial vowel *e*; initial consonants *f* and *r*; initial and final consonant *b*; initial consonant *l*; initial consonant *k*; final digraph *ck*; initial and medial vowel *u*; initial and final *g*; initial *w*; final consonant *x*; initial consonant *v*; initial consonant *j*; initial consonant *qu*; initial consonant *z*; initial consonant *y*; long *a, a_e*; long *i, i_e*; long *o, o_e*